# Find a Penny: A Financial Journey

By

Donna Sako

# Disclaimer

This publication contains the opinions and ideas of its author. It is sold with the understanding that neither the author nor the publisher is engaged in rendering legal, tax, investment, insurance, financial, accounting, or other professional advice or services. If the reader requires such advice or services, a competent professional should be consulted. Relevant laws will vary from state to state. The strategies outlined in this book may not be suitable for every individual, and are not guaranteed or warranted to produce any particular results. Both the author and the publisher specifically disclaim any responsibility for any liability, loss or risk, personal or otherwise, which is incurred as a consequence, directly or indirectly, of the use and application of any the contents of this book.

This book is based on the personal experiences of the author. It is a journal of experiences. It is written to entertain. The author is telling her story of how she began her financial journey and the lessons she has learned during that journey which apply to her. Her experiences and choices are not meant to be taken as legal or financial advice. Each individual needs to make their own choices and seek legal and financial advice from a qualified source.

Copyright © 2014 Donna Sako
All rights reserved, including the right to reproduce this book or portions thereof in any form whatsoever.

Dedication

To my Father, Mother, grandparents and other relatives who taught me through their trials and tribulations. And to my husband who shared my life.

Thanks-Acknowledgements

I wish to thank my Writer's Circle for their inspiration, encouragement, and support.

## Introduction

Saving pennies is how I was introduced to the financial aspects of life. It all began, for me, at age four. Mom was very frugal. She and my father both lived through the Great Depression. As such, they both learned the value of earning a living, spending frugally, saving, and planning for the unknowns in life. .My mother was instrumental in teaching me the basics. Thanks to her and my childhood experiences, I learned how to spend, earn, and save.

When I was 20 years old, I began to experience the challenges of living on my own. Those challenges made me stronger as I educated myself, as required. There was struggle to pay the rent, put food on the table, improving my education, funding medical emergencies, and finding a full time job.

Once I married and had children, new challenges, talents, and strategies were developed. Housing, grocery bills, more medical bills, repairs, and saving for retirement added to my expenses. Errors were made but overcome.

Then came the moving and downsizing of jobs and finally retirement. Life evolved with unexpected highs and lows.

This book a journal of those personal experiences and the lessons learned. After reading a multitude of economic, financial, and professional books on investing, insurance, budgets, saving, and retirement, I realized nobody was showing the reality or results of what really may happen in life. This book is written to entertain and share ideas and information of what I found to be the best and worst of that advice. It is my story of how I began my financial journey and the lessons I have learned during that journey which apply to me.

My experiences and choices are not meant to be taken as legal or financial advice. Each individual needs to make their own choices and seek legal and financial advice from a qualified source. However, viewing things from a different perspective, perhaps learning some new ideas to save, and seeing what may/could happen, might be helpful.

## Table of Contents

Chapter 1
The Foundation
Chapter 2
Applying Control
Chapter 3
Financial Control
Chapter 4
How Do You Spend Your Money?
Chapter 5
How Do You Save Your Money?
Chapter 6
Value for Your Money
Chapter 7
Budgeting
Chapter 8
Grocery Shopping
Chapter 9
The Power of Self Sufficiency
Chapter 10
Entrepreneur
Chapter 11
Stuff Happens
Chapter 12
Dealing with Grief and Finances
Chapter 13
Bad Advice
Chapter 14
Rental Property
Chapter 15
I Did Everything Right
Chapter 16
Variable Insurance by Itself or Within an IRA
Chapter 17

Find a Penny
Chapter 18
Plan B
Chapter 19
Creating That Budget
Chapter 20
Housing and Utilities
Chapter 21
Food
Chapter 22
Gardening
Chapter 23
Recycling
Chapter 24
Health = Wealth
Chapter 25
Job Costs and Emergency Funds
Chapter 26
Retired With Nothing to Do

# Chapter 1

# The Foundation

"Creating a solid foundation on which to build is a necessity." Donald Z. Klein, Carpenter

"A house must be built on solid foundations if it is to last. The same principle applies to man, otherwise he too will sink back into the soft ground and becomes swallowed up by the world of illusion."

--Sai Baba

Find a penny, pick it up, all the day you'll have good luck. For many of us, this is how we are introduced to money. The saying is probably from folklore. Where it began is obscure, but surely during the 1930's Depression finding a penny was good luck- especially when money was scarce. So, it is passed to our children as in play. As children we probably just remember the saying as a game shared with grandparents, aunts, uncles, parents and siblings but later in life it can become a mantra to sound fiscal policy.

I began first grade at the age of five. Beginning at age four, my mother wanted to prepare me for the daily trek to school across two busy highways which I would be making four times a day since I would be coming home for lunch. To achieve this new responsibility I was given a task once a week to run to one of the local mom and pop groceries where I needed to maneuver the streets. I was to buy a loaf of bread or lunch meat or some other item of which was needed and bring the item back with the correct change. Mom would tell me in advance the amount to spend and the amount I should bring home. This was very effective in learning the value of money. But the interesting thing is that on my way back home I would cross a small strip of grass which always contained change dropped from someone's pocket. Found money. No effort, but to pick it up. Sometimes it would be fifty cents on a good day it would be two dollars. But I always found something. So, going shopping for my mom also meant finding money that was for me.

As the years went by, until about age eight, I had a good source of income that was found money. Then as the mom and pop stores died so did my income. I needed to replace it somehow. I managed to talk my mom into doing dishes for ten cents a week. Not much income but it was at least guaranteed. Also, my parents paid me for good grades. I know you probably do not approve of this. But think about it. It was my first job. My job was getting good grades. I got paid once every 6 weeks. So, I had to live within a budget. If I did not do my job I did not get paid. I earned twenty-five cents for A's, fifteen cents for B's, a dime for C's, but nothing for D's or F's. If I could get all A's I might make $2.50 every 6 weeks. I not only learned my lessons but learned the lesson of earning, saving and budgeting. Those real-life lessons are precious.

As I reached the ripe old age of ten, I toyed with being an entrepreneur by running a small local carnival for my friends and family. I offered bingo, over and under, toss games, and much of the usual games which were popular. I had fun and made money from my seed money. I also learned that in gambling only the house really wins. The odds were more on my side than those playing the games. Therefore, I never gambled. I worked too hard for my money to waste it.

Now I know you're thinking, just what kind of a budget does a four to ten year old have? What could I spend it on? Once I foolishly spent a dollar on twenty candy bars making myself sick. I never did that again. Lesson learned-just because you think you want it does not make it worthwhile. Although I did spend some money on swimming, movies, and entertainment, the most fun I had, was when I bought presents for those who loved me and spent time with me during the year at Christmas. I was working mostly to spend on others. I needed very little for me. This is probably where I learned another lesson-living simply and giving was really the most satisfying way to live. Greed just makes you greedier. You are never satisfied because greed can never be satisfied. It is satisfaction which makes you happy. That is what makes a happy life.-being satisfied with each day and moment enjoying life.

# Chapter 2

# Applying Control

"The challenge is not to manage time, but to manage ourselves." - Stephen R. Covey

Find a penny pick it up all the day you'll have good luck. How many times have you tossed that penny or not picked it up because it was "worthless": not worth the effort to accumulate it. When was the last time you had some found money? Money not earned but that just came to you via luck? When was the last time you won at Bingo or Slots? Perhaps won a door prize? Got lucky with a stock pick? You know found money is not worthless. There is no effort exerted to accumulate it. That is why it is called found money. Found money can add up. My pennies as a child probably amounted to twenty dollars or more over a year's time. Anything that you get with little effort is worth getting.

You probably have a change jar at home. If you do not, I suggest starting one. My change jar is where my found money currently is stored. As a child, my change jar was where my earnings were stored along with my found money.

The bank where my parents had their savings account gave them old baby bottles which were turned into a mini bank. So instead of a piggy bank, mine was a refurbished baby bottle. Mom and Dad used to save their pennies in large milk cans. They used their pennies for their Saturday night penny-ante poker games with my grandfather, aunts and uncles. Once they counted the pennies and had enough to pay for a mini vacation. My sons used their change jars as an emergency fund. I still remember them counting each coin and putting them into small piles. Once counted, the coins might be used for gas money. I still see a penny and pick it up. It does bring me good luck, if it is only a sensation I feel, and it helps remind me that fate can bring good things not just bad.

Relying on fate, however, as a fiscal policy is not sound. You cannot rely on fate always being in your favor. My baby bottle was my safe for my earnings as child. But I did not count on fate or my brother's friend opening my bottle and taking my earnings. He took seventy eight cents from my bottle bank. Now that might not seem like much but at 10 cents per week, I lost about a little over 7 weeks of my life and the earnings from washing those dishes.

You need a reliable income to get your bills paid and to have some discretionary spending. This may mean doing a job you may hate at least temporarily. To this day I hate doing dishes. I love my dishwasher. By increasing my income and working toward a job I enjoyed, I was able later in life to avoid the one job I really hate. Now that is power!

Relying on found money or gambling is not very sound either. The odds are against you. Only those who control the game really win. I learned this from my carnival. The object of your goal is to obtain the job of the controller. To do this requires some work. Nothing that is free is truly worthwhile. This sounds like a complete contradiction to the "Find a penny pick it up all the day you'll have good luck" train of thought doesn't it? But it isn't. Remember found money is not reliable. Only reliable money is worth more than found money. Found money is not worthless---it is just not dependable which decreases its worth.

So, how do you become the controller? As I child I ran the carnival, however, I also earned money by earning good grades and doing dishes. So you might want to become an entrepreneur or work a job that pays you a salary. If you are really good at self-discipline and can wait for reward, being an entrepreneur might be for you.

As a child running a carnival or becoming self-employed by negotiating my dishwashing job was a step toward being an entrepreneur. But I would seek some advice through small business counseling if you have no prior experience. Later in life, I ran my own business while working for an employer. That way I was creating multiple sources of income and reducing my risk. Running a small business requires some sacrifice until the business takes off. Knowing that most businesses do not make money for couple of years, I prepared for survival by creating the multiple income sources. Businesses rarely make that $200,000 salary the Politicians keep saying small business owners make. My experience over the last 30 plus years is that most small business owners make less than $100,000 a year-if they are lucky enough to make a profit. So if being an entrepreneur is not in the stars, you will need a job. If you are really lucky you find a job you like, are good at, and that is reliable.

Being a controller is not just earning money. It is finding a reliable safety net. As a child my safety net was my parents. They were the insurance that if all else fails they will bail me out or at least make me feel whole again. As we become adults we must depend on ourselves, but as part of our nature, we need still that security which can make us feel safe. Insurance can help provide that security. Auto insurance, life insurance, health insurance, long term care insurance, warrantees and retirement annuities are all forms of protection for yourself and your family.

I took a Personal Finance course in college. A gentleman, who was married and sat next to me in the class, was disputing the need for life insurance. His argument was: his wife worked and could support herself so he saw no need to have it. I was amazed that he could be so selfish and unrealistic. He forgot that he was living on two incomes. If his wife would die, he would be reduced to one income just like her. If it takes two to run the household then both should have enough health and life insurance to allow the other to survive if one dies. If they have children the financial burden of daycare and raising a child can cost thousands of dollars each year. Protecting myself and those I love from financial ruin is well worth the cost of term life insurance. The younger you are when you get it-the cheaper it is.

Retirement with a pension is no longer a guarantee. I was forced into retirement at age 50 due to downsizing. This also meant I had to take a lower payout than what it would have been later in life. When I retired I was too young for Social Security and not yet eligible for my husband's widow benefit. Social Security does not give enough to be the only source of income once retired. The cost of living increases given with Social Security do not reflect the real costs of aging. The recession and bubbles in the market have increased the need to purchase annuities as a portion of retirement. Much like the lesson of the money stolen from my baby bottle bank, having money saved is not enough. It needs to be protected from the unexpected loss of fate or theft.

Although reverse mortgages are being touted as a retirement solution, I would not enter into them-except at last resort. Why? Because your house may be the last avenue of security you have and last I checked Reverse Mortgages are still expensive. If you do not read all the fine print you could lose your home while you are alive or it may not be available for your spouse or children when you die. They do, however, offer some security when you have little other options left. Reverse mortgages may keep a roof over your head and possibly give you some financial freedom and/or income. Tread carefully.

Health insurance, long term care, Medicare and Medicaid will help with those unexpected health issues that may occur throughout your life and those you love. But even when you take care of yourself stuff happens.

My father smoked since age 5 which probably contributed to his death at age 68. But I had an uncle who never smoked, took care of himself but still developed diabetes and he also died at age 68. I was dieting to improve my health and ate artificial sugars to lose weight but using the artificial sugars triggered autoimmune hepatitis. Fortunately, I am still alive. But fate is quirky. You can do everything right according to the professionals and still have problems.

One of my aunts who had no children saved her entire life and amassed a small fortune. Then she lost her husband and became ill. When she was eight to ten years old, before child labor laws, my aunt took a job at the local tile factory. Years later she went to beautician school and ran her own business. She worked hard and saved all her life. But as she aged she developed white lung from her working in the tile factory when she was young. Her illness forced her into a nursing home. The saddest day came five years later when our minister and her sister had to tell my aunt all her money was gone and she needed to sell her home to pay her medical bills. She died a few weeks' later destitute and heart broken.

My father retired at age 58. All was going well until my mom got sick and put in intensive care for four months. Now one year after retiring he lost his wife. To make matters worse, he received a bill from the hospital alone for a quarter of a million dollars. Terrified, dad called me. That bill alone would cause him to lose everything he worked for all his life. Since my mom was the one who managed the bills and financial aspects of the household, my dad was truly lost. Fortunately, my dad had health insurance which covered all but $30,000 of the final medical expenses which in 1983 was still quite a hefty amount. That amount was equal to two years' salary. The bill he got was before those insurance adjustments. In four short months my dad's entire life changed.

The lesson I learned from watching others is that you need to find a health insurance policy you can afford that covers as much as you can afford. At very minimum get catastrophic insurance with a high deductible but that covers a large life time dollar amount of care. Remember a one million dollar hospital bill at 20% is $200,000 dollars you would be required to outlay. Unless you have enough money saved, your illness can destroy a lifetime of saving. . Getting a policy that pays 80% and you pay 20% is not a bargain. Look for 100% coverage after a nominal deductible fee; say $2,500.

With the Affordable Care Act I believe there is no longer a cap on coverage but out of pocket amounts of 20%, 30% or 40% are still around. Check this out very carefully. The laws change so keep up. You may be eligible for a subsidy from the government if you pay your own insurance and cannot afford the premiums.. That currently depends on if your state accepts that provision in the Affordable Care Act.

Applying control means working, earning a living, and adding security to your life. You can do this by protecting what you have saved or earned from the folly of fate. There are thieves leering at your baby bottles, carnivals luring you to take that unrealistic chance, illnesses, accidents and death are realties we must face. Retirements which flourished into the twentieth century are again fading away. But, if you apply financial control, education, and add multiple sources of income into your life, you may find as I did, that despite all the challenges of life, you can prosper.

# Chapter 3

## Financial Control

"When climbing a cliff, make sure you have a good grip and sure footing." Donna Sako

Do you remember how I began to budget? I saved my 6 weeks grade earnings for Christmas presents or what is known as a long term goal. I also use some of my earnings to start my own business (carnival) to make more money. It only took one bad mistake of purchasing and eating 20 candy bars to realize that lack of control causes pain and loss. I was out $1.00 and had only a stomach ache left over.

As I grew older savings goals became more complex. I had short term (money for the entrance to the dance) and long term goals (Christmas, that outfit I wanted.). I also had unforeseen expenses like having to replace a broken watch or the scarf I lost. So, I needed to set up an emergency fund. Funny how things work out; other kids just relied on their parents as their emergency fund. I may have relied on them for food, most of my clothing, and transportation, but I also needed to prepare for when my parents would not or could not help me. This is a lesson most never learned. I was fortunate to experience the ramifications of my father's 9 month job lapse. Even your most reliable sources of income may not able to be there for you. Take nothing for granted. Prepare for the worst, and you will avoid problems.

Sometimes those resources need you. I remember once when my mom was running short on funds I agreed to an IOU for my grade earnings. She paid me a little at a time when I needed it and she could afford it. No, I did not ask for interest. I did not let greed enter in. Because I did allow the IOU, I not only helped myself get paid, I helped her and the household survive some very tough times. This meant food on the table which I also ate.

Financial control is more than just budgeting. It is being flexible when you are able so that everybody wins. For example: you may be strapped for cash at a time when a friend's spouse or relative dies and really cannot afford to send flowers. You really want to send flowers, but instead, you send a meal or make at least a tax deductible donation to their favorite charity or both. You can show you care in more ways than just sending flowers. In this case, everybody wins. You manage your budget, your friend and you know you care and if you donated to charity more people are helped.

As a child I might have saved $10.00 for Christmas presents but I had 10 people for whom I wanted to buy presents. So, I had to become a very frugal shopper. I was able to buy a kitchen wall plaque, a man's ring, a handkerchief, perfume, a screwdriver, a coloring book, a necklace, a box of lifesaver candy, a jewel pin, and a man's change purse. I also had money left over for bus fare round trip. Not bad for a 8 to 10 year old making 10 cents a week doing dishes and maybe $2.50 every 6 weeks if I worked very hard. I remember my one uncle who got the ring that Christmas wore that ring always and even requested to be buried with it on-and was. So, obviously, I nailed it without spending an arm, a leg, a foot and a thigh. It is not the amount you spend—it is the reason you spend it. Is the reason worthwhile? Does it have meaning? Purpose?

# Chapter 4

## How Do You Spend Your Money?

*The secret of success is constancy of purpose.*
*- Benjamin Disraeli*

It is not the amount you spend—it is the reason you spend it. Is the reason worthwhile? Does it have meaning? Purpose?

Living expenses: Food, clothing, a place to live, transportation, savings, insurance, retirement, emergency fund, extras, repairs, utilities, education, vacation, charity.

Food. This is one area which in tough times you might be able reduce your spending with little effort. I remember my mom taking 2 chickens and making soup, chicken dinner, chicken pot pie, and chicken salad for week for a family of 5. This is where creativity shines.

During a rough time in my 20's, I was upset I did not make enough money to save. So, consequently, I devised a plan to save with groceries. I bought sale items, in bulk, and froze and made ahead dinners whenever I could. The result was I spent less on groceries and freed up money to save.

In college, I took some Home Economics classes because I thought they might be useful in real life. I was right. I did a term paper on supermarkets. What an education! I learned all the tricks and ways to avoid the pitfalls. It was one of the best topic choices I could had make. I learned quite a bit. My husband and I would do grocery shopping together during this time after I got off work at 10 PM. We would go to the only warehouse store around at that time which had all night hours. Together we would apply the tactics learned in the term paper. We began to take a calculator with us and would compare prices between package sizes. Sometimes the small packages were cheaper per unit, sometimes not. We looked for the positioning of products and how that could affect what we bought. Sometimes the sales items were not really sales. It became a game that we were intent on winning.

Therefore, educate yourself. It will pay. I took a Housing Course which taught me how to read a house plan and design one. I learned about where electric & plumbing should go and what makes a good design. This course came in handy when we built our house and remodeled it later. The carpenters, plumbers and electricians found it difficult to con me and the architect learned where his designs were impractical.

The architect's first design on our remodel included a difficult twisted hallway into our new master bedroom. I was able to point out that maneuvering a mattress and furniture through that hallway would be next to impossible no matter how good it looks. He came back with another drawing which was more practical but pointed out the master walk in closet would not be square but 'Y' shaped. I could care less if the closet is square or "Y" shaped. It was a closet. I was not planning to live in it. Actually the "Y" shape was very good. The points on the "Y" split my stuff from my husband's stuff quite nicely and joint stuff was the rest of storage.

We were also adding a laundry closet on the second floor so we no longer had to lug laundry up and down two flights of stairs to the basement. The architect's original plan made it impossible to maneuver baskets of laundry and use the hallway. I wanted more space in front of the closet and if possible no obstruction for hallway traffic. Getting that "Y" shaped closet also gave us the space we needed for the laundry and the hallway.

I also added more hall closet spaces. Next the architect wanted to remodel our existing bath to add a 2x2 foot space into the bath to even up the hallway. I refused. It made no sense and I actually liked the small indented space leading to that bath. It allowed some privacy to that bath and without any added expense.

Our master bath originally included a toilet with door. I saw no real need for it. The shower needed a door but the recess for the toilet was enough. The builder put us on a budget for our tub and other fixtures. He allowed me to shop for those items myself. Despite our $600 budget imposed by the builder, I wanted a tub with a whirlpool big enough for two people. I made some phone calls, researched the web, and made visits. I was able to negotiate what I wanted for the price requested. The builder approached me and asked me how I got the tub for that price since the wholesale price was what I got. You see the tub sold retail for $1700. The builder was a bit upset since he could not pocket the mark up.

I also purchased the tiles for the new master bath and replaced the lower floor linoleum floors with tile which extended into my new home office off my kitchen. I never wanted to replace the floor covering ever again. I added an atrium door to my office so I could have a good view of my back yard as I worked, and therefore, got plenty of light. My office also included an atrium window for plants. I had it wired for a small TV, as well.

The old master bedroom became two rooms. One bedroom for my youngest son and another office for my husband's business. This could easily be used for a bedroom later. But after my husband died I changed it into my exercise room. It now houses my treadmill and sauna.

Since learning from housing course that you should build with expansion possible in the future, when we added our deck we made it strong enough to carry a second floor in case we wanted to expand where my husband's office was or add a second level to the deck. This expansion idea is also why when we added the fireplace when building the house, we added a second flue to the basement. We later added a wood stove in the basement which because of the location heats the entire house in the winter. The stove we bought has a catalytic converter which burns fuel more efficiently and reduces pollution. Learning to think ahead of possibilities was one of the lessons of that Housing course.

When our house was first being built, my husband and I would stop by and review its progress. What the carpenters did not know is that my father was a carpenter. He built his own home. I helped him do it. My father taught me to swing a hammer as early as age 8 and I helped nail the walls and floors of that house. Walking through our new construction, I noticed a wooden beam that had a large knotted hole being used in a load bearing wall. That weak board could weaken the addition of the second floor. I pointed out the board and asked them to replace it with a solid board. They tried to tell me it would not matter. But, the board got replaced.

The electrician was upset that I commissioned two electrical outlets on each wall, lights in the closets, and ceiling lights or fans. He said I did not need them. I quickly explained my uncle was an electrician and helped my father build his home. Having those items was recommended since putting in more stuff later would be very expensive. So, I trust my uncle and my uncle was right when he added them to my father's house. Adding the outlets was costing me $14 each. Later, it could be hundreds.

The plumber gave no complaints after watching me in action with the carpenter and electrician. He actually commented on how logical my choices were.

I took two Powder Puff Mechanics courses to learn how to take care of and understand how my auto worked. I figured at least I could communicate with the mechanic. But it also helped keep me from being scammed.

I was in my early twenties, but I always looked much younger for my age. Although I was 3 months older than my husband, people thought I was his daughter not his wife. In West Virginia you had to have your car inspected every year for safety due to the mountainous terrain. Good brakes on your vehicle was extremely important. So, I was due for my yearly checkup. We can get this done very easily at variety of gas stations or dealerships. Since I just had my brake shoes replaced, I decided to just go to the nearest gas station to get this done. To my surprise the mechanic came out and told me I needed new brake shoes. I got up and walked under my car and onto the small ladder under the wheel where my brake shoes were located. I had the mechanic hand me a ruler. I opened the latch to access my brake pads. After measuring, I began to quote the requirements for safe brake shoes and added that mine had just been replaced and were well above the minimum requirement. Then I said, "There is nothing wrong with my brakes. So either my car passes inspection or we can call the state police." My car passed with flying colors.

What courses could help you to 'LIVE" your life? Making a living is not enough. You must educate yourself on those things which you spend your money. Only by understanding what you spend money on, can you really know if it is: worthwhile, does it have meaning, or purpose.

# Chapter 5

## How Do You Save Your Money?

It is the man who has done nothing is sure nothing can be done.
- Unknown

One penny at time was how I began to save. Later I saved when I got creative with groceries. When I freed up the money from groceries, I saved it automatically via payroll deductions-before I got the check. That way, I did not miss it.

When 401ks first appeared in the early 1970's I signed up. I realized that for every dollar I saved my employer matched my savings up to a maximum of 6% of my salary. That meant by saving I was giving myself a raise! All combined I was saving an amount of 12% of my salary. Then with every raise I just added it into my savings. What I also found was since it was pre-tax I may save 6%, but I always got more in my paycheck as well because I did not pay taxes on those earnings. FOUND MONEY! Remember that? It was just there for me to pick up!

I also had money put into the Credit Union with each pay. They gave lower interest loans and I was a part owner, so reaped any interest earned from those loans. The money did not go to bankers—it went to me and the other members who were lending to each other. It was a non-profit. A win-win.

I did use banks for checking and some savings, but as a rule the Credit Union was more economical because they were not worried about profits. Their focus was service.

When I bought my first house I had to use a bank because the Credit Union was not big enough to handle home loans. However, there are Credit Unions large enough to do so today. So, check around and see if you are eligible to join one.

Another way to save is by cutting your expenses. We all know this. The problem is being able to do so in a meaningful way. The biggest way is to limit your debt. That is a no brainer. That is easy to say--harder to do.

I once was $30,000 in credit card debt. I got there when emergencies occurred and our emergency fund got low. I managed to pay it off in 2 years through will power and borrowing from my 401K. Now, I know, experts say never do this because it will put you far behind in saving for retirement. However, if the debt is so huge you can never pay it off, you will not have a retirement anyway. For me, borrowing at 5% to pay a bill that was costing me 25% was worth it. Also, the interest which I paid, I got back into my account. How? The loan was to myself—not the company. I was forcing myself to pay the principle and my interest back into my account. I did not see that as a loss but a gain. I was still saving my normal deduction while paying the loan as well. Once I did this I got out of credit card debt and never went back. If you have no willpower to pay the loan off in 2 years like I did, I would think twice about borrowing from your 401K. Should you lose your job, that loan is due immediately. If you cannot pay it back, it will be taken from your 401K and you will pay the required taxes and any early withdrawal fees that may apply. It worked for me but not everyone has my tenacity.

One little note: my matching money in the 401k was in company stock. As soon as I was allowed to move it into something else--I moved it. I invested in mutual funds and did not put all my eggs into one stock or basket. This turn out to be a good move later. If you can recall Enron you will understand. Enron employees who kept their 401K in their employers stock suffered huge losses when the business collapsed.

Review how you save your money. Does it make sense? Be flexible if new savings ideas make sense. (For example:

401k) Be cautious if the new product is too good to be true. It probably is a scam. Use that education you have taken to help you make better choices.

## Chapter 6

## Value for Your Money

You have brains in your head. You have feet in your shoes. You can steer yourself in any direction you choose. You're on your own. And you know what you know. You are the guy who'll decide where to go.
- Dr. Seuss

Remember the classes I took in college? Personal Finance, Powder Puff Mechanics, Housing? They not only helped me to get my degree, they taught me real skills I would use my entire life. I once read somewhere where every expenditure should fulfill at least three needs or purposes. If you use this guide you should be able to maximize the value of your money.

For example: The classes I took fulfilled credit requirements for my degree, they taught me life time skills, and the skills I learned saved me hundreds of dollars over the years.

Remember the situation where you were short on cash and a friend or relative has a death in their family? You wanted to buy flowers, but could not afford it? A gift of a donation that you can afford may be given to a charity of the family's choice in place of flowers. Doing so will fulfill your desire to show compassion to your friend or relative, it will fit your budget, and you will be giving to a charity who will help others. The value of your gift will be increased.

Value is also reflected in the wise choices you make with your investments. Make sure your investments:

1. Reflect your values.
2. They are able to meet the goals you have set.
3. They fit into your budget.

Debts should be good debts. The items you go into debt for need to fit the three needs or purposes. Once they are there, the debts should be manageable, cost the least you can get, and be able to be paid off as quickly as possible. The money you save by not paying the 25% or more in interest would be best served being saved than given to the lender. If you can "borrow from yourself" and pay yourself the interest instead, you will stay out of debt and give yourself freedom. I was in debt big time once. However, I made a loan to myself and paid off my debt and paid myself interest. I have been out of debt ever since. To do this requires budgeting.

We will delve into this topic more in detail in later chapters.

# Chapter 7

# Budgeting

*"It is common sense to take a method and try it. If it fails, admit it frankly and try another. But above all, try something." - Franklin D. Roosevelt*

I was fortunate to learn this rather early in life. Without budgeting acquiring your dreams can be difficult or impossible. Being realistic about what you can afford and what you need versus what you want is always a struggle.

Candy bars. Remember them? In those days they were 5 cents each. Soda was a dime, as was a loaf of bread. And what did I do? Yep, I wasted $1.00 on 20 candy bars. My mother was furious. But, she let me learn my lesson by allowing me to "taste" my lesson. I still feel sick thinking about it. The lesson was that impulse shopping was not the wisest thing to do. Afterwards you regret it. You lose your money and the taste for the product you bought. It can literally make you sick.

However, no matter how much you budget, emergencies do occur. I got myself into $30,000 of credit card debt due to emergencies. What kind? Car repairs was the big one. Thousands of dollars in repairs on two vehicles which were needed to go to work. Then, medical bills added on. Include the 25% interest monthly and the 6 years it took to acquire the debt, then because of the large minimums needed to pay, the ability to pay it off became harder. Our income was not enough to make our required bills and pay enough on the credit card to lower it. We were trapped. But, making a loan to myself enabled me to pay it off, lower my interest rate, and stay on budget for those things like food, shelter, insurance. My point is avoid the mistake I did make. Include a hefty emergency fund in your budget. Do not touch it unless it is an emergency. Avoid the repercussions of credit card emergency funds. They are deadly.

What should your budget include besides an emergency fund? Food, shelter, clothing, utilities, and what ever known expenses you have after you have saved for retirement. Those things will be slightly different for everyone. Someone wants a boat fund, Christmas fund, or college fund as additional savings. Others want "fun" fund for weekly movies or entertainment. Just make sure you are realistic and really know what you NEED and provide that FIRST before your WANTS.

I will get more into this topic later in Chapter 19.

## Chapter 8

## Grocery Shopping

If there is no struggle, there is no progress.
- Frederick Douglass

Remember, earlier I mentioned I used grocery shopping to free money for savings? I know you are probably wondering how that occurred. Well, here is the story.

Money was very tight. I just had my second child and my husband was laid off. The good news is he was able to raise the children while I worked. We were now a one earner family. This is normally dangerous to households. Once they get used to spending twice the income because of using both salaries, it becomes very hard to cut back to one salary.

Fortunately for me, I learned very young that you always need a backup plan. Remember the IOUs I allowed my parents? Because of a 9 month layoff my father's normal income was gone. He did odd jobs for neighbors and made wooden lawn ornaments to sell. My brother and I would go door-to-door with my brother's wagon full of lawn ornaments selling them. We were asking $2.00-$3.50 for various ones. What we earned from sales was taken home and used to pay for bills and food. I never forgot that even your most reliable back up plans might not always go smoothly. Back then my parents WERE my ONLY back up plan.

Early in my career I planned. I had a unionized job and was a job steward for 14 years. I lived through threat of strike every 3 years. That made me acutely aware of my father's dilemma when I was a child. So I resolved to learn from it and create backup plans.

What was my backup plan? When we were earning two salaries, we were living on ONE. I pretended that we only had one income and did the normal savings and living off of it. The other income was saved or invested. As a general rule I made more than my husband. So we lived on my salary and saved his. Any increases in pay for me was put into savings via 401K automatically. Therefore, when my husband was not working I had flexibility.

However, children's doctor bills and other emergencies made it difficult to continue saving at the same pace as before. Money was very tight. I remember one week after paying the bills I had $25 to use for food, gas and miscellaneous. Normally food alone was at least $25 a week. So this is when I devised a plan revolving around groceries. I was always a good shopper since the term paper in college but I needed to amplify my results.

I began by buying something I needed and used often but this time I bought in bulk. This meant I would have to do without something else I wanted that week.

Around this time my in-laws were moving to Florida for their retirement. They offered to give us their freezer. It was probably about 10 years old or more but free was worth every penny. We did have to pay for the delivery to my house but I have gotten back ALL that money tenfold. I STILL have the freezer 33 years later. I know maybe it uses more electric to run it these days. But maybe not. I defrost it regularly, take care of it, keep it full, and when I compared the cost of a new one to keeping this one......well the new one lost. Unless I can get another for free that could last another 33 plus years.

This is when the real savings began. With this freezer I could now go to the local Wonder Bakery buy day old bread in bulk for half price or less and freeze it. Day old bread is not "expired" but just one day old. The freezing meant I did not have to buy bread for weeks. That freed up money for other sale items. Now I could take advantage of meat sales.

One of my Aunts was a meat cutter. She and my Uncle had their own mom and pop grocery for several years. I learned how to cut meats into portions I would need from her and my mom. So I could get a whole turkey or chicken and cut it to fry or keep it for roasting. My mom used to grind her own beef for hamburgers and all the stuff you can make from ground beef. I still have my own meat grinder. So the option to use it is there. The less labor required by the store to present the meat and sell it, meant less cost to the meat. I still buy meat in bulk and cut my own steaks, cubed beef, roasts, and can make my own ground beef if needed.

Since I grew up living always near a woods, during the 9 months layoff my dad experienced, my dad would go hunting and we would eat rabbit, deer, ground hog, and squirrel, whatever he could catch. We would go fishing in a nearby creek. Berry hunting was fun and rewarding. Salads could be made of dandelion, wild onions, and other foraging plants. So making use of what I learned in my childhood came flooding back into my life. Plus, many of the things like berries and other fruit that were either foraged or bought on sale could now be preserved in the freezer or made into jams and jellies.

Canning was done more often. My parents always had a large garden. One year, Mom and I pooled our resources and made our own ketchup, relish, canned tomatoes, pickles, applesauce, pear sauce, pickled beets, and sauerkraut. An added plus, we were able to create recipes which were tastier than the commercial products. Our ketchup had a unique tang, thanks to the hot peppers we added. Our applesauce and pear sauces could be made healthier and spiced or not spiced. Canning was healthier and freed more money from the weekly grocery bill.

Gardening became my hobby. When we built our current house, I vowed to garden. Two cherry trees, two pear trees, two apple trees, one almond tree, an asparagus patch, grape arbor, herb garden, and vegetable garden later I am still enjoying my hobby and saving money as well. Harvesting fresh fruit, herbs, and vegetables eliminates the worry of pesticide contamination. You can create your own tastier organic foods and live healthier.

Resisting the sales tactics of grocery stores was easy after my term paper. Especially after realizing that around the time of the term paper canning jars and lids were becoming scarce. After some research, I found that at that time, the same people in control of the production of lids and jars were doing their own canning and selling of produce in grocery stores and they had a monopoly over the canning market. So if they wanted to move their own canned products, they would cut the availability of canning jars and lids. With company mergers, many of "competitive brands" are the same major corporation. They are subsidiaries of a larger corporation but advertising like they are separate. Therefore, the freezer became a way to rebel. People learned to use their jars to create freezer varieties of jams and jellies. Later the frozen foods began to replace canned foods. But now, the frozen foods have added so many additives that making your own and freezing ahead makes more sense and is healthier.

Food producers know that they must extend the life of their products and add chemicals to their product to accomplish that task. Otherwise, their product would possibly perish before it could sell. That would result in a profit loss. But when you grow and freeze your own foods, you can control when and how you preserve them. You control the product, when it is used, and the spices and any other additives. Thus, your food will be healthier, fresher, and meet your needs. You are in control.

Creating my own pantry full of products I bought on sale meant I need not pay full price for the foods I wanted to serve my family. If needed, I can now wait for sales or delay spending for weeks on many items. This meant fewer trips to the store, less money spent and more freedom for my bank account.

Over the years I have refined my shopping by using coupons to reduce costs as well. I do not hoard food. Once I am fully stocked, I live on my stockpile to avoid food getting old.

Learning how my mom and grandma made a chicken last for a week of meals also helped quite a bit. The meat was boiled for broth. Then the broth could be used for flavoring, soup or gravy. The meat could be divided into use for soup, sandwiches, main course, or as a part of other main courses like pot pie, casseroles, or stews. NOTHING went to waste. Left overs became used as soup or other new recipes. Creativity in cooking made us less likely to feel deprived.

Making our own bread, cakes, cookies, and other foods became fun at the same time we were saving. And, moreover, the food was healthier.

This is also when I began to collect cookbooks and experimented in learning how to do more things myself. Doing things myself was more economical.

# Chapter 9

## The Power of Self Sufficiency

"We must believe in ourselves or no one else will believe in us; we must match our aspirations with the competence, courage, and determination to succeed." - Rosalyn Yalow

At age 5 my self-sufficiency was beginning to blossom. My Mom and Dad allowed me to do things myself. The freedom that one learns from self-sufficiency is very rewarding. More so as I got older, I learned that by doing things yourself meant not PAYING for someone else to do them. Skills you learn, no matter how small they may seem at the time, can grow into talents and a career. When those skills become a passion—you may have found your career.

Being able to produce and preserve your own food will give you more freedom of choice in shopping for food. Learning how to repair or make your own clothes will lessen your clothing budget. Doing your own cleaning of your house, laundry, and car can allow you to appreciate what you have; because by taking care of those things, you never take them for granted. When you do not take things for granted you have less NEED to spend money and will probably find yourself a bit happier. Gratitude will reduce your WANTS. Being thankful for what you have will enrich your happiness.

Knowledge is the key to becoming self-sufficient. Notice I have taken many courses in my life which stretched my survival skills. Powder Puff Auto Mechanics, Housing, Economics, Political Science, Sociology, Personal Finance, Courses on Trading Stocks and Bonds, Puts and Options (The ability to hedge your stock bets to reduce losses or increase gains without using or betting a lot of money. Kind of like insurance but seems more like gambling to me at least.), Home Economics, Law and many more had real life uses. The key is to find those things which teach you those skills you will need not just on your job but in your daily life.

Read books. Not just novels but non-fiction which teach you things or give a different perspective so you can make better choices.

Suggested list:

1. Lifestyle/Minimalism
2. Retirement
3. Economics
4. Investing
5. Finance
6. Health
7. DYI (Do it yourself books)
8. Money
9. Physiology
10. Philosophy

Remember the grocery store meats were cheaper if they did not have to PAY someone to cut them up for you. My father was a carpenter. I had uncles which were auto mechanics, machinists, electricians, and entrepreneurs. They shared their talents with relatives in trade. My father shared his skills; they shared theirs. Because they shared, they each were able to build their own homes for less cost. They did it themselves but shared their talents so everyone won. Each had self-efficiency or a talent that gave them more choices.

When you have knowledge or a skill you will have the power to save more. You will become more creative. ***Survivability will increase.***

What knowledge or skill do you have? What do you want to learn? Why? What is holding you back? What can you do to increase your self-sufficiency?

# Chapter 10

# Entrepreneur

"The best way to predict the future is to invent it."
- Alan Kay, inventor

As a child I was always thinking of ways to make money. Found money was the best and easiest. On the other hand, earning my grades was more like having a job. I did on one occasion have my own carnival. Still, even as a child, I cannot see me doing that all my life. Going door-to-door selling lawn ornaments was more working a job although I was donating the wages for a higher good—like eating and paying bills.

When my job became in danger in the 80's, we moved to Baltimore, Maryland. Unable to sell our house while still owing money on it, we chose to rent it out. The rental income paid for the house payment. We were now landlords.

Understand, we fell into it out of necessity. Nevertheless, it became an income stream. It also provided us a plan B should things not work out where we were, and it helped us through some very difficult times as we readjusted our life. (Notice it fulfilled at least three functions?)

Things went along fine until again my husband faced lay off. His company made an offer. If he were to create his own business, he would be guaranteed, by them, to remain as a client for two years. At the time, he was 45 and the ability to find another job was going to be tough.

Now working for my employer over the years provided some education which now became even more useful. I was once given a business office job where I managed my own accounts from beginning to the end. It was like running my own business inside another business. Therefore, I knew how to set up and manage things for my husband. So again, out of necessity, skills that I had learned gave us the ability to survive. My husband kept on doing his job as normal and I ran our business office while I worked full time for my employer. Yes, it could be difficult and tiring but it was worth it. Consequently, now we had two businesses. My husband did his normal abstractor job while I did the billing and collecting and other aspects of running of the business. Our rental property was handled by a real estate firm near our property. This freed some of my time to run the abstracting business as required.

Other income opportunities brought other forms of income as well. When the opportunity came we managed to have the talent to take advantage of it.

Being in business for yourself requires help. You need a lawyer, accountant, and insurance agent. Read some books on it. We incorporated to protect ourselves. I did the books with the help of good software and an accountant. This is when we also got Personal Liability, business and other insurance to protect the assets of our home. We borrowed from our savings to start our business and paid our savings back BEFORE we took any profits or wages. That way we reduced our risk. Because I always banked my husband's wages and lived on mine and I continued to work, this also lowered the risk. He was guaranteed at least one client for two years so we had time to expand with less risk as well.

Keep in mind that most businesses fail in the first two years. Small business owners may not take a salary for years from their profits. So if you must borrow money, know what you need to live on and borrow enough to **pay you a wage**. This is one thing many forget to do. We did not need to worry about that since I was still working full time and we were living off my salary anyway

Our business was successful. Both of us retired at age 50.

# Chapter 11

## Stuff Happens

*"The truth does not change according to our ability to stomach it."*

-Flannery O'Connor

Funny how a crisis will spur things along. Twice due to necessity we fell into business on our own. But the road is not always smooth even when you think you are doing fine—stuff happens.

Yes, we retired at age 50 but again it was not by actual choice- but necessity.

My husband required heart surgery. With an arrangement I made with another business, his business would continue while he was being healed. During this time, I was able to work my normal job from home and take vacation days as needed to tend to him. He got well and all was fine until about one year later. He was having more difficulty managing his work. He applied for Social Security Disability and retired. Nine months later he passed away. During this time frame, my job was in jeopardy with cut backs. I had almost 30 years in service and could retire. The company made a retirement buyout package which included healthcare for me and I retired as well about six months after my husband died.

Now begins the trials and tribulations of retirement. Things were fine until I got bored. So I reopened my husband's business and changed it into a consulting business. I could use my work experience to help others in that field and took a part time job as a business consultant at the same time. Later, I joined the local chamber of commerce where I later was hired as their executive director for eight years and then retired again. During the chamber job I had to choose between my own business and the chamber since my time was becoming stretched. I chose the chamber and closed my business.

During those years, I experienced the issues which occurred from 2001-2011. The mortgage bubble, the wars, market crash, and job scarcity. Which brings us to the next few chapters.

## Chapter 12

## Dealing with Grief and Finances

"After climbing a great hill, one only finds that there are many more hills to climb." ~Nelson Mandela

As a job steward and management, I watched the reactions and effects of many of my peers who lost their loved ones during my career. Back then companies would give you about three to five days to mourn and then you were expected to return to work. If you had vacation time coming you could possibly take some extra time on top of that but were always expected to return to work and go on as "normal".

The reality of it is, things are never "normal" again. Grief has a tendency to leave you feeling lost, alone, and not quite on your "normal" game. But to the outside world you must act like things are "normal". I knew this from watching others; when it hit me—it hit me hard. But like it or not back to work and acting "normal" was required.

Pretending to be "normal". That is what is required. Just like in the past, when things are out of your control, you must muster the strength to go forward. It is not easy. You will still be hiding your emotions when at work. Then cry as you drive the lonely commute to home and quietly sob yourself to sleep each night. Things will happen that remind you of the missing link in your life. However, you will muster every ounce of will and strength to move forward. You cannot change the past, but you <u>can</u> move forward.

One issue, moving forward, would be the settling of any estate which occurred due to the death of your loved one. That takes months or years depending on how well your loved one planned ahead. There could be medical bills and the threat of bankruptcy because of them as well as your own depression with which you may have to face. During this time, sadly, there are many people who will *prey* on you not *pray* for you.

The first to come is the funeral home and its bills. They will try to make you feel guilty if you do not give the "best" send off for your loved one. Even a modest funeral is in the thousands which you might not have. So while you are alive I recommend a discussion on the topic. Life insurance to pay the bill or will you set the money aside like an emergency fund? If you can afford it, save the premiums instead of giving them to the insurance company to cover this, that would be the less costly—if you began saving for it early enough and NEVER touched it. But like most people life insurance is probably what you have at the minimum. Social Security will pitch in about $200 for burial. That has not changed for decades. $200 might actually have paid the bill in 1933.

Fortunately for me, my husband and I had discussed it. We both chose cremation. It is far less expensive and more flexible. Cremation has been a choice most of my father's family had made for decades. So it was natural for me. My husband liked the idea and requested it as well. I did have two small funeral services or gatherings once his remains were returned. One in our home town of our youth with family and the other with friends in our new residence. This gave some closure.

Next the insurance companies will give pay outs but "advise" you to reinvest with them. Sometimes this is a good idea—sometimes not. Vet them very carefully. They will have many "ideas" for you. Some are helpful but they are still trying to make a sale.

Then comes the attorneys, court system, tax department, creditors which include the medical bills, and anyone affected by a will or estate. Fees. Lots of fees. Everyone seems to profit from fees. Hopefully a will and/or revocable trust was established. Retirement accounts-especially IRAs need to have TOD (Transfer of Death) as part of the ownership so upon death it will automatically transfer without probate. A will takes care of the miscellaneous. The revocable trust might transfer property directly without fees to your heirs. Joint ownership of property with spouses will also pass the property to the survivor. Try to keep as much out of probate as possible. This will avoid fees and allow the estate to be settled quicker.

As an executor of my father's estate earlier in my life, I learned much of the perils of settlement. The fees can take a great deal of the estate funds. If someone contests the will the settlement can take years and lots of fees to resolve. The estate could be greatly reduced and in some cases wiped out due to bickering. It was a learning experience. In addition, as an executor, I had to adhere to the law. That made at times hard feelings. One's ability to bend is taken away which many beneficiaries do not understand.

If you are the executor, you can hire an attorney to work for you for the estate. But if choices can be made, you will be in the position to make them. Joint executors could ease the burden as long as the executors can get along. So when making your will make sure you choose carefully. Executors get to charge a fee so try to avoid an attorney directly handling the estate. Why pay them twice?

# Chapter 13

## Bad Advice

"Each of us wages a private battle each day between the grand fantasies we have for ourselves and what actually happens." - Cathy Guisewite

"Value is also reflected in the wise choices you make with your investments. Make sure your investments reflect your values, they are able to meet the goals you have set, and they fit into your budget. "--Donna Sako

Thirteen has become the omen of evil. The killing of the Knights Templars occurred on Friday the thirteenth. As far back as the Norse God Frigga according to Wikipedia it has been seen as bad luck. So bad advice is appropriate for this chapter.

Remember the insurance companies? We had life insurance on both of us that should either of us die our debts would be paid and there would be money left to help the survivor carry on for years until social security and pensions would kick in.

The plan was to pay off the house, bills, and invest the balance wisely to live on. But remember grief? Well, grief clouds our judgment. Although I am relatively aware of being frugal and money wise, when grief kicked in it wanted more attention than anything else. Just thinking about financial issues was taxing. I was a mental wreck. So I made the mistake of allowing bad advice to enter into my life.

Paying off the house would free monthly income and allow me to save more. But the insurance company advised I not pay off the house but invest the money instead. That way I could deduct the interest on my tax return. After all, I could make more money in the market than I pay in the house interest. Yep, sadly, I fell for it. The reality was the profits were not guaranteed but the house interest costs were. I was guaranteed via the house loan to lose 9% in interest costs every year. What was I thinking? I wasn't.

After a few months, I did refinance the house loan and reduced the interest to 5 ¾ %. That was a mildly sane moment. Unfortunately, the lender sold my loan to a larger bank who was located in Texas. Now, because the bank was out of state and Texas laws took over, my escrow would no longer pay me interest on the money they held. That really burned. Now they had access to my money and did not have to pay anything for that access.

My husband had a small IRA account which I inherited. The bank was losing money on the investments so I wanted to move the money. My employer had an investment firm come in and offered to transfer my money to them to invest. Again, I was gullible. After I did this I was discussing with their advisor about my stock options. I was given the options which allowed me to buy the stock at $43 a share which at the time of issuance was lower than the market price. But at the time I was talking to the "advisor", and she wanted me to cash in my options, my options price was now a great deal higher than the stock price. The price was now $18 a share. If I exercised my option I would LOSE money. I would have to pay $43 for stock being sold at $18. This is when the light bulb finally went off. She was only interested in my money and her fees. I quickly moved my money into my Variable Annuity IRA.

I can hear you now. Variable Annuity IRA? Yes, they have fees. But they are also carry life insurance on principle at the highest point in five years. (Or so I thought). Yes, I bought this after my husband died. In the Variable Annuity IRA, I could let it grow, get money from it when I needed, or later take it as an annuity and was also guaranteed 3% interest on any cash I had invested. I did not have to annuitize until age 95 and could cash it out well before that age if need.

Recently I have read that our emotions effect the choices we make. Boy was that right. If you are dieting and feeling sad or stressed you eat more and have a harder time staying on your diet. When you are highly emotional, you are not thinking clearly and can make bad choices and listen to bad advice.

Listening to the bad advice gave me little value for my money. The choices offered did not reflect my values, rarely met my goals, and endangered my budget. My temporary insanity of grief carried a high price tag. Be cautious especially if you are grieving.

# Chapter 14

## Rental Property

Start by doing what is necessary, then what is possible, and suddenly you are doing the impossible. - St. Francis of Assisi

The house we rented out was paid off. It was giving us a small income stream monthly. Then, in 2005, upkeep on the property was costing more than the rent we charged. We hired a realtor early on who took care of the property and collected the rent for us. In 2005, the realtor was retiring and no longer going to act as our agent. It would be very difficult to continue renting the property from a distance. Also, my current house needed repairs and upkeep. With the prospect of mounting costs, it became necessary to sell the rental property.

My tenant bought the property. I would be the bank. This would have worked out fine except the tenant who was to pay the taxes and insurance was late with those payments. This meant I could lose the entire income from the property when the state would foreclose for back taxes.

I paid the taxes and collected the money from the tenant, but after that scare I did not want to gamble anymore with that income. Fortunately, I began to get offers from investment companies to buy my mortgage income. (This is what my old bank did to me. They sold my loan to another bank.). So after, some legal issues. I sold the property loan for what I paid for the house when we first bought it. At least I broke even.

This brings me to lessons learned.

1. Rental Property is a good investment if you can live near enough to the property to maintain it or have a company or person to manage it when you are living far away.

2. If you are going to maintain the property be sure to set up an emergency fund, funded by part of the rental income, for unexpected large expenses like a new roof, new furnace and other future maintenance. Rental fees should be increased to fund this. I kept the rent low and did not keep up with possibility of large costs. I think I did this because I thought I might move back into that house later in life. (Again emotion.)

3. If you become the bank, it is worth it to collect an escrow account in addition to the monthly house payment to ensure you maintain the taxes and insurance and do not lose the house income for those fees not being paid.

4. Good news is there are companies who will purchase your house lien income and rid you of the stress in managing the loan.

5. If I had gotten the escrow, I might be collecting income for 15 years. But, I let my attorney talk me out of the escrow account. Again BAD ADVICE.

## Chapter 15

## I Did Everything Right

"Experience is not what happens to a man; it is what a man does with what happens to him." – Aldous Huxley

In 2001 the stock market was doing ok until September 11, 2001. Then the market took a drop due the attack in New York. One week later my retirement began. Within 6 months, I lost my husband, my job due to retirement, and the stock market dived. My entire life changed overnight.

All my working life I saved, invested, and cared for my family. We had done everything right. We were college graduates, owned rental property, bought a house, owned our own businesses. We took care of our health and raised our children to be good citizens. All the lessons I learned from childhood seemed to just fade away. All the work, worry, and accumulation of talent and planning could not stop fate.

Now I had to start over. Just a year ago my husband was alive. I had a steady job. My investments and future looked bright. But now, I felt I was back to zero.

What I **did not do** was panic. I did not remove my money from investments. I kept a large emergency fund and began to use that instead to allow my money to grow back. I did not sell my rental property until fate forced me. I reduced my expenses and reopened my husband's business as my own consulting business. Since interest rates dropped, I refinanced my house loan to lower my monthly costs. I found a part time job at the same time I did consulting. In other words, I fought back. I picked myself up and went forward.

How many times have you been kicked in the gut by fate? If so, I hope you have the courage and strength to fight back. When fate happens, it does not mean you have lost. It means you need to change course. Find other paths toward your goal. But, never, ever give up. Always keep an eye on your goals and watch for barriers. Go around them, through them, or over them. If you do, your chances through persistence or tenacity to reach your goals will greatly be improved.

My investments were held in a nice mixture of funds. I took a course on investing and Puts and Options (The ability to hedge your stock bets to reduce losses or increase gains without using or betting a lot of money. Kind of like insurance) to increase my odds in my favor. The courses were worth it. They allowed me to understand the market a bit better so I could make better investments. However, what I learned about hedge funds, puts, and options was that they were not for me. They felt more like gambling than investing. I wanted to invest in business not gamble. I preferred mutual funds. But, a mixture made up of different industries. I read the prospectus of every one of my investments and looked at which companies they were invested in. If I found too much invested in companies I did not like or felt were unstable I moved money to another fund. I did this faithfully.

During this time frame, I joined the local chamber of commerce and later became their executive director for eight years. It was a part time job which allowed my investments income to grow.

Then in 2005 I was noticing the housing market was askew. Interest rates, the loans, the market did not look right. This is also when my issues with rental property were happening. So I felt it was a good time to sell that property. That was a good decision. Selling it then, even though all the issues with the house payment and taxes I went through, freed me of hefty potential losses. By selling my property in June 2007 and later the loan to the investment company, December 2007, I secured at least a break even on my investment. With the crash which began in 2007, I am not so sure things would have worked out.

The money from the sale was used to make repairs on my house and beef up my emergency fund. This became extremely valuable in 2008.

Financial Crisis 2007-2008. The crisis began to be noticed in 2007 but the crash came in 2008. I got out of the rental business just before the crisis became more critical. My emergency fund and part time job allowed me not to panic. I could allow most of my investments to grow back. Still in the fall of 2008, I had lost $200,000 on paper in days. That would have paid off my house loan at least twice.

I had done everything right. I invested properly according to the classes I had taken--but still in days I lost many thousands of dollars. At least, I was prudent enough to have a hefty emergency fund.

As the market came back, I ended up losing about $80,000 at last count. Why? Because after this crisis I realized I had to pay off my house. I could not chance another crash while paying a house payment. Doing so would mean paying taxes on my IRA withdrawals and those withdrawals would mean less money to earn back my investment.

Realizing I would be 59 ½ soon, I began to make a plan to pay off the house as soon as possible. Once I turned 59 ½, I withdrew fifty per cent of what I owed on the house in fall of 2009. Then another fifty per cent of the remaining balance in January of 2010. Then in January 2011 I paid off my house. By spacing payments this way, I was able to manage the taxes. In retrospect, I should have paid the house off in 2001 when I wanted. But, I allowed bad advice to seep in due to grief. Now my sanity was slowly coming back.

The biggest lesson I have learned is that you cannot control everything. You can do everything right and still find yourself in a quagmire. Fate has a way of creeping up on you. Because you never know when fate will happen, you must always prepare for the worst and have a plan B, C. and D.

# Chapter 16

## Variable Insurance by Itself or Within an IRA

*"You can complain because roses have thorns or you can rejoice because thorns have roses."* Ziggy

According to most, if not all, books I have read concerning this investment option this is the worst type of investment.

A variable annuity is an insurance product which allows you to invest your money but will at the same time offer life insurance. The thought being, that after a period of time, your account will grow and then later insurance will freeze and if the market collapses just before you die, your heirs will get the higher amount of the insurance policy. Unusually there is a minimum required wait time before you can withdraw money 7-10 years. Each policy provider has different requirements so it does require you to plan ahead long before you need the money.

- Like other annuity products they start out as tax-deferred. But when you withdraw your money you do not receive a tax deduction. But then again neither do you when you withdraw from you IRA unless it is a Roth IRA.

- The commissions and fees can be high. But then, so is the cost for life insurance especially as you age. The greater the odds the insurance company might have to actually pay—the higher the rates.

- Investment options are limited. Most have a selection of investments from which to choose. It will not be the entire market.

- The life insurance only kicks in IF your account is lower than the amount of its original value. So, it is not in addition to your accounts value. As you withdraw funds the life insurance is also reduced. I found this out after I began to withdraw money for paying off my house.

- Annuities are disadvantageous to inherit if they don't go to a spouse. I think this is a tax issue for others. So that life insurance included with a variable IRA or annuity is not really taxed like life insurance. It is still treated like an IRA. The insurance never is tax free like most life insurance policies.

- Disclosure to individuals is complex and can be evasive. When they are making a sale much of the fine print is left out of the discussion. If you do not know what to ask, they do not tell.

- Variable annuities are not liquid for years. Withdrawal rules can be complex. It makes no sense if you need the money now to live.

- Because they work similar to IRAs any previous after tax money will convert to a higher taxable amount. They are not much different than IRAs.

So, why did I buy one?

- Since this was around the time of September 11, 2001 when stocks took an unexpected dive, the insurance part was looking good to me.

- I could name my sons directly as beneficiaries.

- I was only 51 and would not need the money for the next 7 years which was my waiting period.

- It was being funded by money from my previous employer as part of my pension and I was required to roll it over into an IRA or Annuity to avoid tax issues.

- My variable annuity would guarantee 3% interest forever in any cash I invested and still allow me to invest as I might want.

- I did not have to annuitize until age 95. But, could withdraw money as I needed.

- Originally, this was to be my medical expense emergency fund.

Well how is that working?

- After the main investment, I later took my husband's small IRA and moved it here as well. Those combined monies earned a 66% profit over six years.

- Even during the crash of 2008, I never lost my principle.

- By 2009, when I began to withdraw funds to pay off my house, I had still retained a 25% profit.

- When interest rates tanked to less than 1%, I created an emergency fund of 2-3 years of living income earning 3%.

- Now, if there is a hint of another crash, I can stop selling stocks from my other living income source and use the emergency fund here instead. That will allow my stocks to recover and reduce my losses.

Although this may be a bad choice, I found a way to make it work.

- What I did not realize when I bought the policy is that as I withdrew funds from here, my life insurance amount would be reduced by the maintaining per cent I secured in life insurance—I did not retain the larger dollar amount. My $183,000 of life insurance was reduced to $59,000 as I withdrew money to pay off my house. Knowing this now, I do not expect to add more funds into this account.

- If I add any money into it, those funds will need to be held for another 7 years. I am now too old to tie up my money. So this will continue to be an emergency fund.

## Chapter 17

## Find a Penny

When you run into debt, you give another power over your liberty.
- Ben Franklin

Find a penny pick it up all the day you'll have good luck. Remember this from chapter one? Now it is time to do a little review.

We have come a long way from age 5 when finding loose change was a beginning. From found money to earned money. From applying control to losing it. From obtaining value for your money to making the best you can from bad choices. From joy to sorrow and then somewhere in between.

Life is about doing the best you can with what you have. Learning and experimenting along the way. As easy as it is to pick up that penny it can all be lost in an instant. No matter how much you try to control everything-- not everything is in your control.

So now we begin to discuss those plans B, C, and D.

When I was a child my father had a plan B. When he was laid off he began to think outside the box. As a result my brother and I were selling lawn ornaments door-to-door. My dad was doing odd jobs and projects like repairing or tarring roofs. He began to hunt for food and increased his garden. Plan B needs to be something that will take care of immediate needs until things become normal again. That can be an emergency fund, or other multiple income sources. <u>Avoid debt as your emergency fund.</u>

Plan C, is what you do when Plan B is no longer feasible. This could be insurance policies, investments, or more dire last resort emergency fund accesses.

Plan D, is the worst case scenario. This could mean filing bankruptcy, selling your home or other assets. This is where little or no choices are left.

I prefer to have a strong Plan B. Having such will give you more control and choices. But it might require some sacrifice. You might have to cut back on spending. That means no more lattes, going to movies, or entertainment for which you spend money. It might mean more meals at home, increasing your garden supply, and canning and freezing your own food. You might have to mow your own lawn, paint your own house, do your own repairs, and get creative. But, what it might do as well, is educate you to what is really important in your life. You might become closer to your children or other relatives and friends. You might, in some cases, find out who your real friends are. Moreover, as in my case, you might find that Plan B is where you really want to live.

# Chapter 18

# Plan B

"Perhaps all human progress stems from the tension between two basic drives: to have what everyone else has and to have what no one else has." - Judith Stone

The one who dies with the most toys...still dies.
- Unknown

Before we can begin Plan B we need to discuss the difference between being self-sufficient and greed. Why? Because it will have a great deal to do with your choices and how you will survive. It will challenge your character and ethics.

Stock market crash of 2008. When many investment companies were living the high life, they never created a Plan B until the last minute. They were seemingly gambling with money that was not theirs and had little conscience in doing it. Because they were used to gambling and not really investing in companies, on a daily basis, they had made themselves <u>numb to loss</u>. They had to do so in order to continue their life on a normal basis. So when they were faced with requiring a Plan B many did as they have always done. They sold products knowing full well they were bad in order to maintain their image and survival. They did not seem to care who they hurt as long as it was not them. Their commissions and split second gambles, in some ways, were fixed. They created machines that could figure the odds of loss and allow them, ahead of the normal consumer, to know the "real" cost of the investment and instead of using that knowledge for their clients, they used it for themselves. They had created an environment where they could not lose. Or so they thought.

As a consumer do you make choices which allow you to live the high life? Have you created a system that is more of a gamble than reality? Do you consistently spend money you do not have using the machine of credit? After all, if you always pay part of the bill each month you can continue living your life at the level far higher than you can afford. Are you numb to the possible losses you can have? Are you now at the point that you have no choice but continue this practice to survive? Are you fooling yourself into thinking the only one who will be hurt is you? Did you forget your wife, husband, and children? How will your actions affect them? If you are single, what about the friends you have borrowed from? Or the people you hurt if you do not pay your bills? Yes, not paying your bills might cause other people to lose their houses, jobs, cars, or investments. **What you do, whether you are a company or just yourself, ripples into society.** Your desires, much like the desires of Wall St, are similar.

Plan A is what you do when you think no one but you will be affected. It is the instant gratification of "wanting what everyone else has and to have what no one else has." This sounds a little like greed doesn't it? But it isn't unless it goes to extremes.

So now let us compare Plan A with Plan B.

In Plan A, the accumulation phase, you desire what everyone else has. A job, a house, a car, perhaps basic living needs like food, utilities, entertainment, and all the daily pleasures you can buy. You also want to have what no one else has, a better job, a house, a car, better food, entertainment, and you can afford those utility cost increases. And definitely more daily pleasures than you need.

So you start earning money with a job. Perhaps you begin just earning enough to pay the rent. Might not have a car, your apartment might be furnished so you have very few possessions. But you crimp and save the best you can. Your desire for a better life requires more money. So you eventually find a better job. Nothing wrong with improving yourself. But you find as your job earnings improve there comes a point where you no longer have the time to do things for yourself. So you hire others to do those things for you. When you do this, you are taking a pay cut.

Think about it. What is the real cost of your job? At one point I was working 70 hours a week as management. I got, if I was lucky, five hours of sleep each day. I had a three hour commute daily. I had to purchase a wardrobe that fit the job. I had to spend money on gas and transportation to get to my job. I had no time to pack a lunch, so I ate out. I used my vacations to do upkeep on my house since I used about half of my earnings *just* to maintain my job. Despite this somehow I managed to save enough to retire by age 50.

Although I was living in Plan A, I had a Plan B for emergencies. I had the emergency funds for the unexpected. We had multiple income sources via rents, investments, and business ownership. But we had also a large credit card debit of $30,000. That happened because of <u>amount</u> of emergencies which happened. Our emergency fund was not big enough. But, I did have a backup C which allowed me to pay off my credit cards, save interest, and remain out of debit.

So while you are living in Plan A make sure you create a Plan B. It should include several safe guards.

- A large enough emergency fund to cover two to three years of wages. This needs to be in an easy access form. It could be a savings account, Money Market, or something that pays some interest and your principle is safe as possible. Most experts say six months to a year should be saved in case you lose your job. But if you have multiple issues hitting you at once, as I did, that is not enough.

- If you are paying a high mortgage rate, look to refinance to a lower interest amount and reduce your loan payback time. Despite the professional's advice, paying off your house will give you great peace of mind and free up the interest money and those payments to invest, save, or create a more solid emergency fund.

- Make sure you have good insurance for your home, car and health.

- If you can afford it, look into buy a Long Term Care policy when you are young. I bought one when they first came out in the 1990's through my employer when I was in my early 40's. Once I retired it was transferable to me personally at the same rate I had under my employer. It was very affordable and cost pennies compared to those offered once I aged into my 60's. Because I did this, I can still afford the policy.

- Life Insurance costs rise as you get older and closer to death. So you are probably better off getting Term Life when you are young. As you age or retire your life insurance needs diminish. Unless you can afford the many thousands of dollars on a yearly basis for a policy, it might be better to just set the premium costs amounts aside for your own funeral. Especially if you have no one left depending on you to survive. The older you are the greater the odds you will die, therefore, the life insurance rates are higher because now insurance companies might actually have to make a payout.

- Make a will and consider a revocable trust for your house for transferring your property. Power of Attorney and Medical Advance Directive should also be considered at any age.

- Hone your skills and education to create more opportunities should Plan A be a bust.

- Create multiple incomes for security.

- Watch closely for changes in the law which might affect your life and the choices you make.

- Learn more about Social Security, Medicare, Medicaid, Family Planning, Food Stamps, and any other help agencies in case you need them. These are like insurance policies for you. **You have paid taxes into these over the years so if you ever need them they could be there for you. Support them and remember <u>you could be one fate away from needing them.</u>**

## Chapter 19

## Creating That Budget

You have to dream before your dreams can come true.
- Abdul Kalam

I purposely did not get into the details of this in Chapter 7 because I wanted you to see how things can change over the years. Yes, there are basic items within your budget you must have, but they change yearly and by decades. The budget I set at age 5 will not work at 63. My main point is, you must learn to be flexible with your needs and wants. Yes, both need to be budgeted.

When I was first on my own at age 20, I worked part time at two jobs just to make the rent. Fortunately, that included utilities and was furnished. I had no insurance. No car. I walked to work. I did grocery shopping once a month using a taxi. Yes, I was on food stamps for about a year until I landed a well-paying full time job. I used Family Planning for my healthcare. They did not cover everything of course so I needed to keep myself healthy. Once I did get strep throat and went to doctor nearby who was able to give me antibiotics as part of his fee. However, I did take vitamins and the walking gave me plenty of exercise.

I was also within walking distance of the college I attended. Wanting to continue with school but not having the funds, I got my first student loan. While in school I did not have to pay it back, so this was not in my budget as yet. But I knew I had to find a job that would allow me to pay it back later.

During this phase of my life 92% of my income was budgeted to rent. The $10 monthly I had left was for the taxi ride and miscellaneous expenses I might have. But I tried to save even then.

Once I got the good job, my first action, after the 6 months trial period past, was to begin to pay off my student loan. I was able to pay it off in 18 months. Once making a decent salary, I was no longer on food stamps. I, now, had to add more food costs into my budget. During this time, I also added to my savings. Then about a year later, I bought a car. This increased my budget in the form of added insurance and car repairs. Life and health insurance was offered via my job so I had that deducted from my paycheck. So now I no longer required Family Planning. As my life expanded so did my budget needs.

As you move through life your budget will ebb and flow much like the tide. Your needs will rise as darkness comes and wane as the brightness dawns. You goal is position yourself so you will not be drowned by the rise of the tide. During the ebb you must make your plans in a way to protect yourself from the tide. Trying to do so while under water is dangerous and could drown you. Occasionally you might experience a tsunami. So you need to watch for those signs. The farther you are away from the flow, the safer you will be—even from the tsunami.

So how do you budget? First look at your needs.

Housing-this includes the utilities.

Food

Health

My father served in World War II. He was a gunner and spent much time in foxholes. After that experience he used to say, "All you really need to be happy is a roof over your head, a full belly, and a warm place to shit". I apologize for the S--- word but it is my Dad's quote.

But not being healthy or taking care of it can ruin your life. Being sick is not fun and the dollars you spend can make you bankrupt.

Therefore, having a place to live and the expenses to live there, food to sustain you and keep you healthy, and insurance or access to healthcare are the basics.

Once you have a job, transportation costs may need to be added. If you are lucky to have a job within walking or biking distance great! You will save money and increase your health.

Jobs usually require a style of dress. It could be a uniform you are given or a business style of dress, or if you work a trade blue jeans might be ok. But the need *for* and upkeep *of* the dress will need to be added to your budget.

Depending on where you work, you may either pack your own lunch or eat out. They both require budgeting. If you can bring your own lunch you will save quite a bit. If not, this will increase your job costs and lower your salary. Remember**, *the costs to maintain your job, less what you earn, will give you the true hourly wage you are earning.***

Being a job steward for 14 years, I learned that if you add your work benefits on to wages you earn, you might find a clearer view of what you are earning as well. Not many people look at the added value of those interests. Some companies offer to pay two thirds of your premiums on health insurance. You find this our later if you buy under COBRA. This could mean thousands of dollars. Vacation time, IRA matching, life insurance, dental, vision, and more all add up. So keep this in mind when you look at your budget. What would those costs be without those benefits? Then use **those** figures to help you with creating a better emergency fund into your budget.

Where are we now in our budget?

- Housing—rent or mortgage payments
    1. Utilities—phone, gas, electric,
    2. Food------groceries
    3. Health—insurance or access to care
- Job costs--
    Transportation---car, bus, train, bike, walking, taxi, gasoline
    1. Clothing requirements
    2. Food requirements
    3. Car insurance and the cost to maintain the car

- Emergency Fund
    1. Should include what you would lose if your employers stopped paying for it.
    2. Should include a minimum of 6- 9 months of lost income.
    3. Should increase to 2-3 years of living expenses to ride out a bad stock market in lost income.

As your life gets complex so will your budget.

Children will increase your amounts required in your budget for food, health and probably housing as well the children's needs and wants. Your need for life insurance, childcare while you are working, toys, education costs, and transportation cost will increase. Last I read a child can add over $200,000 per child in costs over the 18 years you are raising them. That is a huge chunk of your budgeting. But we love them anyway. Our lives would be less meaningful without them. But you will need to consider them in your budget.

As we buy our houses, now we need to care for our lawn and property as well as the house. This can mean riding lawnmowers, tools, plants, seed, and possibly farming that out to others to do if we are living at our jobs 70 hours a week. Those costs are added to the budget. Also house repairs and maintenance might be added.

Then come the wants. The things. The toys. The bling! Those items which you feel you just cannot live without. I need my latte at work—several times a day. I need that new phone, style of clothes, the new game program or TV. We really need that 1000 foot addition to our home or the pool. The list goes on.

Now here is where the rubber hits the road. <u>This is where your budget is working for you or you are working for your budget.</u>

This is where many people really fail. They buy stuff just to make them feel good or to keep up with the Joneses. They will be living in an altered universe where there are no repercussions for their actions. The credit card comes out and ALL sanity is lost. For me, it was not the wants that hurt me. It was the needs. It was the lack of a big enough emergency fund to cover those unforeseen needs. But for others I knew it was the wants. That extra latte, the Rose Bowl Ticket, the Gym Membership they no longer used. It was wanting more than what others have.

Greed. I am not talking frugal. Frugal is not the same as greed. Frugal people spend less on some things so they can spend more on other things. It gives them freedom to spend money on the really important things they value. No greed is the desire for instant gratification, with little to no thought about the thing but that desire. Greed does not care about budgets. Greed does not care about the results of the actions greed makes. Greed is selfish. It only cares about that thing or desire that makes it feel powerful-if only for a short time. Greed may not need or deserve what it wants but it does not care.

If you need a new TV buy one. If you want it to be High Definition and Smart and you have the cash for it without going into debt long term. Great! If you do not really **need** a new TV but just want one with the new stuff, and, in order to get it, you must go into debt at 25% interest for years, since you will never pay it off in the one year you promised yourself, **no, do not buy it.**

This is where will power is required. I might like a new freezer but the ones they make now do not last 33 plus years. The freezer I have is working fine. I take care of it. It meets my needs. Every television I have ever owned each lasted well over 10 years. I only upgraded when the old one died. Replacing things just to have the newest style or functions that I may or may not need is a waste of money and is not environmental. The new devices may not only-not last as long- but are much more expensive and may cost more for upkeep. **Instead of leaping to your desires have the patience to wait.**

Tablet computers and e-readers have become more fashionable. As our cell phone morph into mini computers, our "need" for computer flexibility in software increased. Books could now be read on a handheld device instead of a paper book. Since using less paper is more environmentally friendly I did take an interest. But the cost of buying a tablet was almost as high as my desk top or a lap top computer. Also, at the time, I did not have access to Wi-Fi.

Then one wonderful Christmas my eldest son bought me a modem and hooked me up to Wi-Fi. I was so happy I cried. His thoughtful gift now made owning a lap top more worth it. I could now use the lap top not just as a lap top but I could attach it to my TV and get video.

The following year I replaced my XP desk top computer. (XP was no longer to be supported even though my 2003 computer worked fine. The computer was also in need of more hard drive space. So it was time to replace considering the costs.)

Since I was now a member of Amazon Prime and using the access to films and free shipping, I also got an offer from Amazon concerning a Kindle Fire. They were offering a price reduction to $99. This took my interest. So I clicked the e-mail link. I reviewed the offer. Then I remembered that if I applied for their credit card I would get $50 off my order. I also had some Amazon Gift Certificates. Once these were applied as well as my free shipping, my new Kindle Fire was $35.91. This is now a want that I could afford and could justify. I was afraid to pay the full price since I was not sure if I would like it or not. The risk was not worth the want. But by waiting, I eventually got my want.

This is an example of frugality not greed. If I let greed in, I would have paid the higher price just to please my gratification and not waited until the want became an opportunity.

Now about that credit card. I basically use it occasionally mostly on Amazon. I have no annual fees and the interest rate is average. I also earn Amazon points which I can redeem with Amazon purchases. I pay it off after each purchase.

The biggest challenge you will ever face when creating and maintaining your budget is yourself.

Sticking to a budget takes dedication. In order to do that, you may have to give up, delay, or reduce the wants to take care of your needs.

## Chapter 20

## Housing and Utilities

*The one person you have to watch, if you're going to save money, is yourself.*
*- Unknown*

We are still working on your budget. But I thought it would be nice to have those basic parts which make up the budget have their own chapters for easy reference.

What kind of housing do you need or want? You need to be realistic. Our first home was a small two bedroom house with a one bath, a stand in kitchen, a dining room and living room. We had a full basement which included a section for the laundry area. Later my husband made part of it his computer room. At first it was just the two us and one child. Then we had a second child. We still managed but it was a bit small. It was our starter home. What we could afford on my income. It had some wants. It had one wall which was a bookcase in the living room. That sold the house for my husband the book collector. For me, I did not mind the small stand in only kitchen. It made it easier to cook. The house had hardwood floors as well as carpet. But it was not a mansion.

Most financial experts tend to advise your house payment should be less than 28 to 35 per cent of your take home pay. I definitely agree. Even less if you can manage it. Have a heavy down payment to reduce the amount you borrow and find a way to pay it off as quickly as possible. Having a guaranteed roof over your head in case you face a financial tsunami is worth it. Negotiate the lowest interest rate you can. If you must accept a higher rate or are stuck in one now, refinance to a lower rate as soon as you can. Again work on paying the loan off as soon as possible, so go for 15 year loan or pay extra on that 30 year loan.

Once you are able to pay off your home, use the old house payment money to create more savings, investments, and a larger emergency fund.

Make your house as energy efficient as you can. Utility bills can eat your budget. Gas and electric costs keep rising. Make sure your house is well insulated. I even have insulation in the electrical outlets on my outside walls. My attic access has an insulated dome which covers the opening of the stairwell. Ceiling fans, automatic thermostats, shutting off lights as you leave the room, turning off electrical devices or unplug them when not in use. Look for energy saving electronics when you need to replace them. Keep the refrigerator and freezer full and with the right temperatures. The money you save will reduce your spending and give you more flexibility with you budget.

Water usage can derail your budget. So keep your toilets and sinks and other plumbing in good shape. Lower your water heater to 120 degrees or I have heard of timers for the water heater for when you are sleeping or long periods of non-use. There are also water heaters that heat as you use it and do not require a tank. Do some reading and investigate your options.

As a Competitive Intelligence Specialist with Verizon, during the beginning of the competitive era in telecommunications, I became familiar with how competition in what was once a monopoly market works. My experience there helped me to work with a power aggregator during the competitive era of energy where I created an Energy Co-op for the chamber of commerce. Energy Co-ops are a means to reduce energy costs to your home or business. I belong to the co-op and have managed to save hundreds of dollars a year through them. So you might want to investigate one near you. An aggregator will look for the best price among those who might serve your geographical area and recommend who has the best offer. You could do this yourself if you have the knowledge.

In telecommunications that market is growing and changing every day. My best advice is to research what is best for you at the price you can afford. Internet and television may be included. But unless the laws change or the market, air waves for TV are still free for the basic channels. Now days many are cutting landline, the cable or satellite and using their computer connections along with the air waves. You can have land line or mobile phones or both. The options seem to be growing daily.

Your goal is to continually reduce these fixed costs as much as possible so you can pay them even during a financial tsunami. That can mean that you review them often. At least once a year.

# Chapter 21

## Food

The best place to find a helping hand is at the end of your own arm.
- Swedish proverb

Read Chapter 8.

Depending on where you are in life and who you share your life, this can change. When I was young Chapter 8 freed money for savings and other expenses. But now I am retired. My needs are less. I no longer am feeding a family of four seven days a week. I am proud to say I still keep my grocery costs as low as possible. But these days I am even more into health.

Health = Wealth

When I was in my early 30's I went on a diet where I used artificial sugar instead of sugar. Suddenly I was having digestion issues. The artificial sugar killed my natural bacteria in my system. Fortunately, eating yogurt put the bacteria back.

Then in my 50's, I again used another artificial sugar, only this time, I even baked with it. After a few months, I was feeling weak and developed jaundice. This scared me. After tests and evaluations, the artificial sugar is what caused my issue. It had triggered autoimmune hepatitis. My family has a strong history of having the arthritis gene. That gene was activated. But Instead of arthritis it manifested a false condition which caused my body to attack itself. The artificial sugar tricked my system into thinking my liver was the enemy and my antibodies began to attack my liver. Medication was prescribed to reset my system. Once this occurred, my body healed. It worked. Since that scare, I have been eating only natural sugars and more natural foods. The condition could re-occur if I did not remove the artificial sugars from my diet.

As I continued to read in books and on the internet about the GMO's, which are changing our foods genetic makeup, I keep thinking how the things we eat, which may be altered, may not be recognized as food by our bodies. Our system might begin to be tricked into fighting diseases when it is not a disease but the unnatural foods.

I have also read that when our bodies do not recognize foods or substances we eat, that it may be stored as fat. I am not sure why our bodies do not eject it outside of our bodies but it this is "food" for thought.

Therefore, even more than for financial reasons, I create my own jams, jellies, can my own food, freeze my own handmade frozen dinners, make my own yogurt and bread and buy as little processed foods as I can. It is not only more frugal but healthier.

My vegetable garden, fruit trees, grape arbor and berries I grow give me exercise as well. This is a hobby that fulfills at least three functions. Financial health, healthier food and exercise for strength.

Make sure you are looking at foods and your environment. These can contribute to your health as well as your budget

# Chapter 22

## Gardening

*Few things come to him who wishes;
all things come to him who works.
- Unknown*

In my youth I began gardening to reduce my grocery bill and free money for other things or to save. As I have aged gardening has become a hobby I enjoy. My yard is a Certified Wildlife Habitat. Watching the plants grow and the animals flourish fills me with life as well.

I enjoy the creativity gardening can provide. The beauty of a flower garden. The joy of watching birds, squirrels, chipmunks, rabbits, and other wildlife from my back deck. My father taught me to always grow more than you need so you can feed nature as well. That way both can co-exist; creating that balance in nature.

With the growth of mass commercial farming, that is lost. Instead of working with nature, the commercial farmers get greedy and work against nature. They create insecticides, and GMO crops, and worry more about their bottom line than the health of nature they are attacking. As such, unhealthy substances have entered our food supply. Honey bees are dying. No one has a good reason why. But what if it is that by changing the molecular structure of our crops that has changed the pollen and nectar composition? Now the honey is tainted. The bees eat the tainted honey. Bees die. Then we eat enough of that honey along with the other altered plants and we die. This may not be true, but again, "food" for thought.

If man has domination over the earth and animals, then man has the **responsibility** to ensure the health of all creatures and plants--not just man. And the little quirk is, that if we *do* take care of the creatures and plants, then nature is in balance and we all survive.

Grow an herb garden. Here are tons of books and information on how to grow one and how to harvest, preserve and use them. My herb garden is full of spearmint, oregano, thyme, chives, rosemary, lavender and other spices. I make my own mint tea, mint oil, and dry my own herbs and spices. I am planning to add more creativity.

Creating beauty and joy from gardening enriches your life. It will bring you in balance and allow you to be grateful for the blessings you do have. Once you feel grateful, you will find the having more is no longer a need. You will have obtained all that you were really searching for all along. Happiness.

# Chapter 23

# Recycling

When your outgo exceeds your income,
your upkeep is your downfall.
- Unknown

Along these same lines, recycling is another project worthwhile. I have a composter where I can create my own healthy soil. Since our community is into recycling waste, I have found by separating the paper, glass, and plastic from my garbage that my garbage is significantly reduced. Again I am using the NOTHING goes to waste mentality which with I grew up.

Find ways to reuse products that wear out or seemingly have no use. Or find alternatives in your life that make more sense environmentally as well as for your pocket book.

Did you know that lint from your dryer is highly flammable? I save the old toilet paper tubes, fill them with lint and use them as fire starters for my wood stove in the winter.

Old spice bottles can be used to store your homegrown spices or the products you make from the herbs. Oils and extracts can be made and stored in them as well. Or create other storage ideas like for your workshop nails or screws. Why buy a container when you may already have one? Get those creative juices flowing!

Lightly rusted bread pans you have replaced can be painted and used as flower pots or other storage containers. Old cookie sheets can be used to hold or carry things. Egg cartons can be used to start seedlings as well as tin cans. Old ketchup or mustard bottles can hold the homemade cleaning supplies you made.

Mow your own lawn. Use a mulching mower. You will lessen the need to buy fertilizer which has chemicals that my harm your water supply.

There are books on alternative cleaning supplies which are cheaper, healthier and work just as well as the costly, chemical laced products on the market. Vinegar, baking soda, salt, cornstarch, toothpaste, vegetable oil, lemon juice, aluminum foil, and bleach all are cheaper and have a variety of uses. The internet is full of ideas and options.

I have my own mulching machine. When I trim the plants, trees, and shrubs around my house, from the larger stems of trees I create fire wood. The smaller branches and stems are mulched and used in my yard around those same trees and plants. What cannot be mulched at home, I take to the city for recycling.

When I trim my grape arbor, the vines, I can use for mulch or I can make them into vine wreaths which may be made into gifts or sold.

With imagination you can greatly reduce your waste and save money as well. I do realize that if you are working 70 hours a week instead of retired, that doing all these things for yourself might not be possible. But if you have the time, it is well worth it.

## Chapter 24

## Health = Wealth

"So many people spend their health gaining wealth, and then have to spend their wealth to regain their health."---
A.J. Reb Manteri

Health Insurance and taking care of your health is the third main requirement in your budget. If you cannot afford healthcare seek out agencies or non-profits who can provide you those services. Without your health your ability to make and retain any wealth is difficult. Health costs have been one of the major reasons for bankruptcy. To protect what pennies you have managed to save, you need to find a way to stay healthy.

Remember, one of my aunts saved all her life. Once retired she thought she had enough saved to live out her life. Then her husband died. She got sick and was taken to a senior care facility. After five years, her sister along with her minister had to break the news to her that all her money was gone. She had to sell her home and everything she owned. The news broke my aunt. She died soon after.

Medical expenses even with insurance and other retirement sources can take everything away if the financial tsunami is big enough.

This is why just having health insurance is not enough. You must keep yourself healthy. Stop smoking, over drinking, and abusing your body. Ask questions about the drugs doctors want to give you. Are there homeopathic things you can do that can prevent or ease your issues instead? Get second and third opinions. One doctor cannot know everything.

A few years back I was bringing in groceries and I had a severe pain in my thumb. It felt out of place. So I went to my doctor. He reviewed the situation and declared I had arthritis and put my thumb in a brace. He ignored my insistence it was out of place. The brace never worked so I removed it. I was suffering with this for six months when one day as I lay in my bed my dog took an interest in my thumb. He was smelling my thumb and suddenly smacked his head as hard as he could against the thumb! PAIN! But suddenly after that pain hit, the pain went away and I could move my thumb! My dog knew what my doctor did not. Since then my thumb has been back to normal.

Take the responsibility to care for yourself while you have your health. Prevention is worth a pound of cure. Solutions do not always come from the professionals.

My husband developed diabetes at 35. He did not take it seriously. I took courses on how to cook for him to try and keep him well. But I could not be around him 24/7 and he had to take responsibility. Then at 48, his health got worse. He had a stroke, heart surgery, developed an infection, and then I suspect he was over medicated. A little over two years later he died.

When I became ill I made changes in my diet and am much healthier today than many of my peers. I am told I look 5-10 years younger. I have energy and strength. While I may have good genes, they cannot keep me alive if I do not cooperate.

By staying healthy you have more money. You do not need to spend hundreds or thousands of dollars each year on medicine. Your budget and your body will thank you.

# Chapter 25

## Job Costs and Emergency Funds

You can't have a better tomorrow if you are thinking about yesterday all the time.
- Charles F. Kettering

Within the previous chapters we discussed how job costs can skew your real salary and how your emergency funds should include those benefits dollars from your job. Now I would like to share how I came to those conclusions.

Remember how I struggled working two part time jobs with making just enough money to pay my rent? Once I was working full time I never forgot those lean times. Although, if need be, I could go back to a furnished efficiency apartment and eking a living, I never want to do that again. Living on food stamps is not the joyful, greedy existence that many political pundits preach. Having to pray for your next meal or that you can avoid a catastrophic illness is not the life you want to live. You live every day in fear. Fear of becoming homeless. Fear of sickness and death. Fear of safety.

Once I was working full time I made a vow to NEVER go back to that life. This meant I had to be diligent in every aspect of my life. Thinking about a better tomorrow and not dwelling in the past. Not forgetting the past-just not allow myself to dwell there.

To increase my odds of survival I became a job steward. This was more than survival for myself. Because of the sparse life I led before this job I also did not want anyone to live that life. Empathy for those individuals who were stuck in that environment and wanting to help others have a better life were also a factor. It was during this time as I helped write, read, and enforce the contracts made between the union and management. Despite what others may think, as a steward, I was required to adhere and enforce the contract. This meant occasionally in favor of management. *I was a mediator.* I looked for win/win for both sides while making sure the contracts were enforced.

It was during one of the strikes that it "struck" me. When we negotiate these contracts much of our income was in benefits. If we did not have those benefits, we would need to pay for them ourselves. Companies can negotiate better rates in insurance than an individual. That benefit is passed to the employee. Without that ability of mass, no individual can compete. But if those benefits would be lost, you would take a large pay cut. This meant that sometimes benefits were of more value than a large wage increase.

Now let us assume you lost your job. COBRA costs are astronomical. When you cannot pay for them, you are without the safety net health insurance gives. To make sure you can survive you must have enough of an emergency fund to cover those costs until you can find another job with benefits or a better/affordable policy.

Strikes were occurring every three years. That meant that for three years you had to plan for another strike. If all you do is plan for a strike it makes it hard to live your life. Slowly the unions began to realize that fact. Now strikes have become rarer. This is good for the businesses and for the employees. Balance helps both sides to win.

Then a management job was opened to me. But, it had risks as well. As management I had little voice about wages or recourse if I felt I was being treated unfairly. But I do earn higher wages, a few better benefits, and a little more freedom.

Since the risks have changed, I now needed to re-evaluate. My emergency fund would need to replace my new salary, insurance, and a much larger amount of job costs.

Then as my husband got ill and my ability to care for him waned. My job requirements hindered my ability to care for him so, I began to re-evaluate my financial life again. By this time my savings, emergency fund and investments were much higher. Retirement was popping into my head since I was getting close to 30 years of service.

Once my husband past away, the actual hourly wage vs the job costs sunk deeply into my mind. Rumors of management Reduction In Force (RIF) were becoming louder.

I attended company meetings discussing the RIF and the offers the company was making. After much forethought, I awoke one morning and said, "Enough". Not that I had enough. It meant, when is enough—enough? How much more do I need? What more must I do to survive? What kind of life do I want?

I did not want to die doing the work I was doing. So many of my co-workers had died without retiring. I personally knew at least 10. The racehorse I was on only had so many races left. I wanted to change which races I ran—and retired.

Now retired, I no longer had to travel to work, buy lunches, dress in clothes for the job. My budget dove. Gas for the car went from $1,560 a year to $360. Lunch every year went from $3,000 to ZERO. Clothing cost went from $2,000 a year to $300. I saved $6,200 a year.

As my children grew and became self-sufficient, I no longer needed to pay for insurance for them. And as I found even more to cut each year I became happier. I had less stress. My emergency fund does not need to be quite as high because my bills are lower.

Every year I continue to reduce my expenses. I am **living** more.

## Chapter 26

## Retired With Nothing to Do

"Minimalism is the promotion of things I most value and the removal of everything that distracts me from it."- Joshua Becker

When I first retired at 50 my feelings were a bit mixed. Having freedom to sleep in every day if I wanted and taking time for myself were greatly welcome. Along with those came days of loneliness since my husband was not around. I missed the comradeship of work. Now I had time to catch up on the household chores. For three months I cleaned, de-cluttered, and sorted through my life. I painted and did some Feng Shui throughout my house to make me more relaxed and comfortable.

After about three months, suddenly I was bored. I began to take Tai Chi, Yoga and other classes. I joined the Y and did water aerobics. I took tap dance lessons. But my mind was used to being active. I decided to reopen my husband's business and do consulting.

Things were going well. I enjoyed the part time work mixed with the other activities. Then I began to do my gardening again. I was amazed how happy this made me. As a youth I spent a great deal of time in the woods enjoying nature. I had forgotten how much I missed that part of my life. The simplicity of just enjoying each moment instead of meeting a deadline was powerful.

The local chamber of commerce needed an executive director. Since this was a part time position and, like my old job steward days, it would give me an opportunity to help others on another level. I applied and worked there eight years. This job was very fulfilling. But as I aged, I found I wanted more freedom.

Then after 2008 and the crash, I knew I had to pay off my house and really retire. I made a plan to retire by 2012 and did so.

Now, I am really retired. We have a library within walking distance to my house. I began to frequent it more often. My gardening increased. I found that my needs were much less.

Once your house is paid off, almost one third of your income is free to save or spend. Now that less people share your home, you use less utilities. You still need health insurance but only for you and perhaps your spouse. Your clothing budget is almost erased. With those costs reduced, you have less stress. Less stress means you relax and begin to revisit what you really enjoy.

Minimalists live on less because they find they do not have the need for things others crave. I just recently realized that is what I am becoming. Minimalists are quite happy living on less with less stuff. Having less stuff means saving money and having to spend less time taking care of that stuff you really do not use, want or need. I am slowly beginning to remove anything that does not give meaning, purpose, fulfillment, or lasting joy into my life.

When your life is full of "stuff" it can distract you from finding what really makes you happy. You begin to realize that experiences are more valuable than things. You find yourself to be more giving. Envy goes away and gratitude grows. When you feel more gratitude, you feel happier. Instead of chasing the next newest thing, you become happier chasing butterflies. The earlier in life you realize this, the richer you become both financially and emotionally throughout your life.

Cooking has been rediscovered. Recently I bought a pasta maker and have begun to make more of my own creations. All the cookbooks I have collected over the years are getting more used since retirement. Making more of my own food instead of eating out saves me money and may keep me healthier.

My grocery shopping costs are down. Maintaining a pantry has helped me to lower my weekly bill to $35.

My hobbies give me plenty to do. Fortunately my hobbies save me money as well.

Boredom is no longer felt. I have found ways to keep my mind and body active.

My father once told me that after he retired he was busier than when he was working. But he was happier because he was doing more of what he wanted to do.

Saving enough to have the freedom to live your life in the way that really makes you happy is your goal. You might not be happy doing what I do. But whatever you do, plan ahead. Make adjustments along the way and try to avoid financial tsunamis. Life is to be lived; not bought or owned.

About the author.

Donna Sako was raised in Wheeling, West Virginia and is currently living in Taneytown, Maryland. She earned her Bachelor of Arts Board of Regents Degree in 1977 from West Liberty State College which is now West Liberty University. Her studies included Social Science Comprehensive, Home Economics and Law. In 2001 she retired from Verizon Communications. She owned and operated Alpha Research, Inc. and served as Executive Director of the Taneytown Chamber of Commerce. During her working career she also served as a Customer Service Representative, Small Business Counselor, Consultant, Teacher, and Competitive Intelligence Specialist.

www.ingramcontent.com/pod-product-compliance
Lightning Source LLC
Chambersburg PA
CBHW071519040426
42444CB00008B/1713